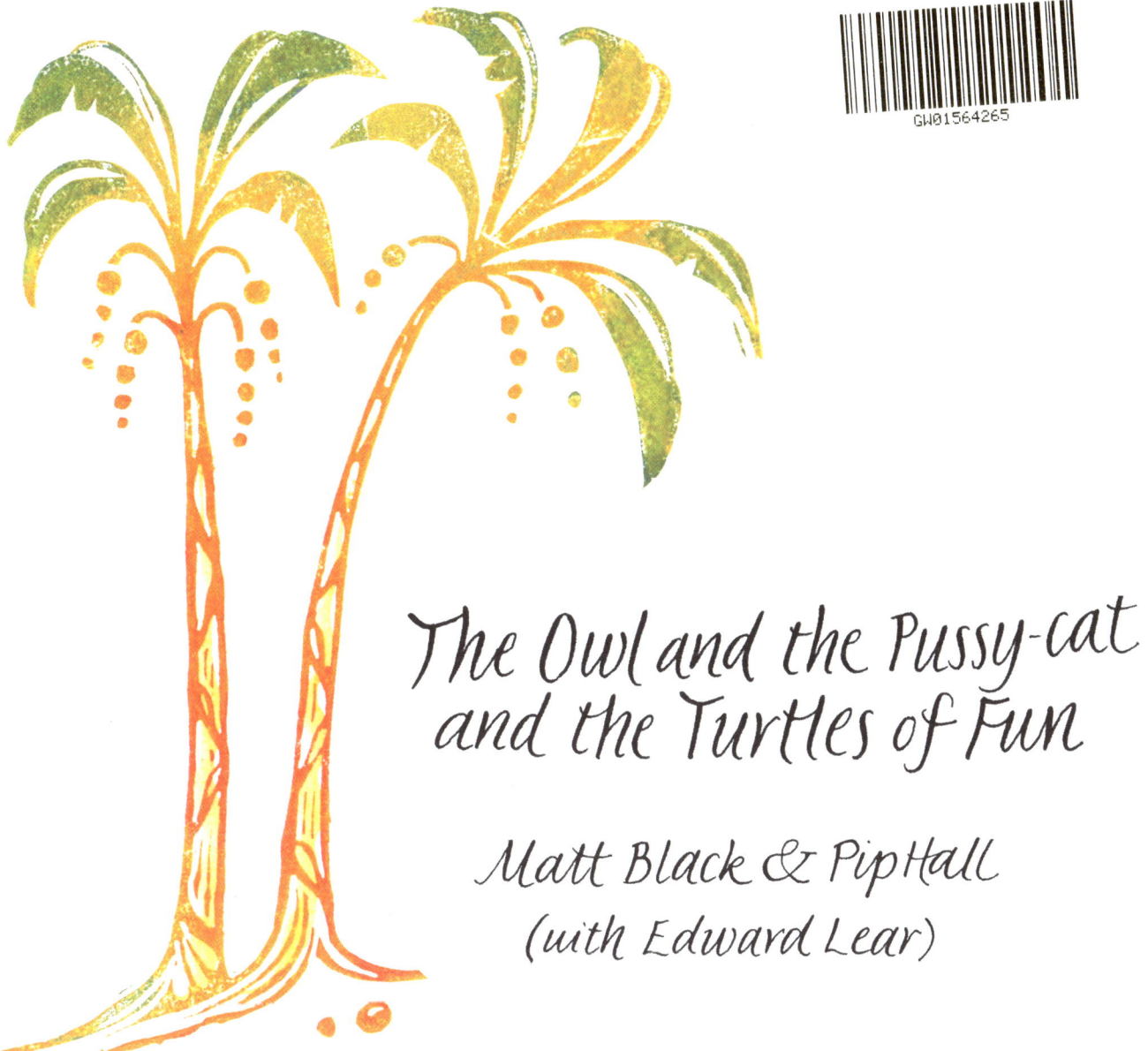

The Owl and the Pussy-cat and the Turtles of Fun

Matt Black & Pip Hall
(with Edward Lear)

ALSO BY TWO RIVERS PRESS

Places and Other Poems by Thomas Hardy
The Ballad of Reading Gaol by Oscar Wilde
Cat Jeoffry by Christopher Smart
Kubla Khan by Samuel Taylor Coleridge
Spring Song by William Shakespeare
Winter's Song by William Shakespeare
Sumer is Icumen In by an unknown medieval author
The Drunken Boat by Arthur Rimbaud

First published in the UK in 2014 by Two Rivers Press

7 Denmark Road, Reading RG1 5PA.
www.tworiverspress.com

Copyright © in The Prequel and The Sequel Matt Black 2014
Copyright © in illustrations, lettering and design Pip Hall 2014

The right of the poet to be identified as the author of The Prequel and The Sequel has been asserted by him in accordance with the Copyright, Designs and Patents Act of 1988.

All rights reserved. No part of this publication may be reproduced, stored in or introduced into a retrieval system, or transmitted, in any form, or by any means (electronic, mechanical, photocopying, recording or otherwise) without the prior written permission of the publisher.

ISBN 978-1-909747-03-6

1 2 3 4 5 6 7 8 9

Two Rivers Press is represented in the UK by Inpress Ltd and distributed by Central Books.

Cover design, lettering, illustrations and design by Pip Hall (with acknowledgements to her neighbour's cat).

Printed and bound in Great Britain by Ashford Colour Press, Gosport.

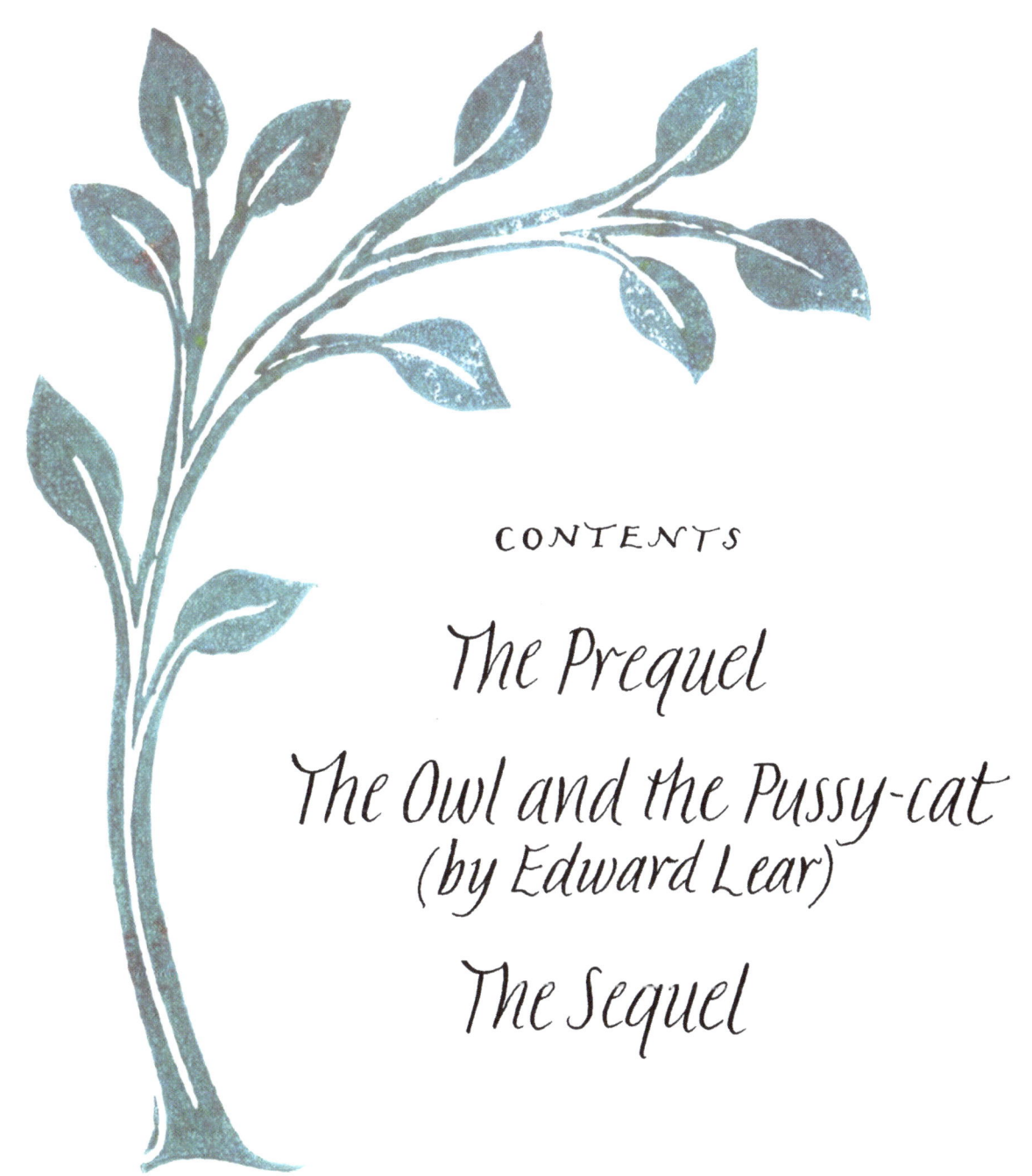

CONTENTS

The Prequel

The Owl and the Pussy-cat
(by Edward Lear)

The Sequel

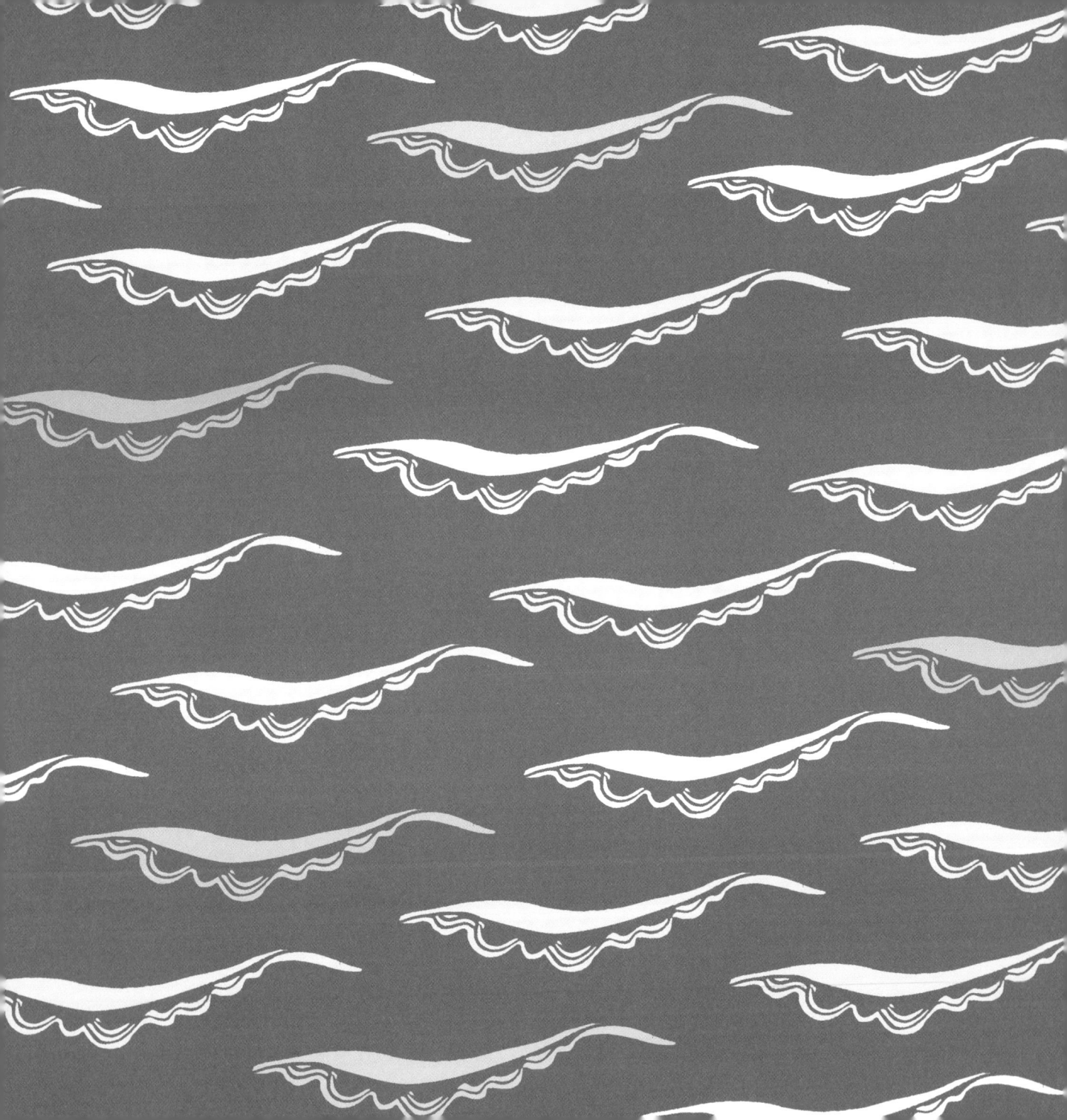

The Prequel

The Owl and the Pussy-cat went for tea
With a parakeet in the park.
Owl said politely,
'It doesn't delight me,
This hunting of mice after dark.'

The Cat said
'Life in the city is mean;
We're squibbling youth away.
Let's go to the sea.
Let's quit this mad scene':

So they cycled to Brid for the day,
The day,
The day,
So they cycled to Brid for the day.

With a sailor who told them a tale
Of a mermaid and man,
who had met in Japan,
And lived in the mouth of a whale.

'I like it here,' said the Owl on the pier, while the Cat, with a grin, went 'Miao'.

They stayed for a week.

They played hide and seek,

And the Owl jumped over a cow,
A cow,
A cow,
And the Owl jumped over a cow.

The waves, they were lapping,
blue butterflies flapping,
'O guys,
you should stay for a while.

'We've striped candyflosses,
and rides on the hosses.
It's wicked whatever your style.'

Said Cat 'Life's absurd.
Let us sail, dear Bird
To the land where the Bong-tree gleams.'
In his crocodile coat,
Sailor lent them a boat,

And said 'Steer by the star of your dreams,
Your dreams,
Your dreams.'
He said 'Steer by the star of your dreams.'

The Owl and the Pussy-cat
(by Edward Lear)

I.

The Owl and the Pussy-cat went to sea
In a beautiful pea-green boat,
They took some honey, and plenty of money,
Wrapped up in a five-pound note.
The Owl looked up to the stars above,
And sang to a small guitar,
'O lovely Pussy! O Pussy my love,
What a beautiful Pussy you are,
You are,
You are!
What a beautiful Pussy you are!'

II

Pussy said to the Owl, 'You elegant fowl!
 How charmingly sweet you sing!
O let us be married! too long we have tarried:
 But what shall we do for a ring?'
They sailed away, for a year and a day,
 To the land where the Bong-tree grows.
And there in a wood a Piggy-wig stood
 With a ring at the end of his nose,
   His nose,
   His nose,
 With a ring at the end of his nose.

III

'Dear Pig, are you willing to sell for one shilling
  Your ring?' Said the Piggy, 'I will.'
So they took it away, and were married next day
  By the Turkey who lives on the hill.
They dined on mince, and slices of quince,
  Which they ate with a runcible spoon;
And hand in hand, on the edge of the sand,
  They danced by the light of the moon,
        The moon,
        The moon,
  They danced by the light of the moon.

The Sequel

The Owl and the Pussy-cat
lived the dream
For a year and a half at least.

They built a chalet,
and pranced in a ballet
On the beach with the Jumbly Beast.

Till Pussy-cat met the Turtles of Fun,

Left Owl by the frumious foam,
  Who sat in the sun,
    cried 'What have I done?
  O and why did I leave my sweet home,
      Sweet home,
        Sweet home,
  O and why did I leave my sweet home?'

Now six months have gone,
and Owl's signing on;
Cat lives with a Turtle called Ted.

In the Bong-tree bazaar,
Owl strums his guitar,
Singing 'Pussy,
my marriage is dead.'

But Cat, in surprise,
 says 'Owl, do be wise,
For love is a runcible fruit.'

The Whiskery Walrus
and Octopus chorus
Heard songs, like the Dong's, on the sand.

'Your tunes are so beautiful,
groovy and hootable!'
Begged Walrus,
'O please' join our band.'

Owl pondered and said,
'Yes, but only if Ted
Can play drums and the didgeridoo.'

They made Number One, with the Turtles of Fun,
Singing 'Life is a crazy canoe,
Canoe,
Canoe,'
Singing 'Life is a crazy canoe.'

For Anna and Maya PH

In celebration of extended, improvised and made-up families, everywhere. For the runcible fruit knows best. MB

Matt Black lives in Sheffield and Leamington Spa, writes for adults and children, and enjoys working with musicians and other artists. In celebration of Edward Lear's bicentenary he wrote *The Nonsense Olympics* (Upside Down Books, 2012). www.matt-black.co.uk

Pip Hall runs a lettering arts studio in Cumbria. In celebration of twenty years since she was involved in the first Two Rivers Press book, *Where Two Rivers Meet*, with fellow founders Pete Hay and Adam Stout, she is pleased to produce this book with Matt Black. www.piphall.co.uk

Edward Lear (1812–1888) was the father of nonsense literature, famous for his limericks (There was an Old Man of Peru …), and for poems such as *The Dong with the Luminous Nose* and *The Jumblies*.

Two Rivers Press has been publishing in and about Reading since 1994. Founded by the artist Peter Hay (1951–2003), the press continues to delight readers, local and further afield, with its varied list of individually designed, thought-provoking books.